God is everywhere, everywhere.

> ~ Jan Zwicky, Songs for Relinquishing the Earth

For abiding is nowhere.

> ~ Rilke, Duino Elegies

The singing of the wolves is not to him the dreadful sound that it is to some. The wolf and his song are as much a part of the wilderness as...himself, for they are hunters too, and suffer from cold and hunger, and travel long hard trails, as he does.

> ~ Archie Belaney, Pilgrims of the Wild

Also, by Denis Stokes

Scarborough Poems *(Wordwrights Canada)*
Dublin in the Sunlight *(Albernum Press)*
With Adam, Gathering *(Albernum Press)*
What the Street Knows *(Albernum Press)*
Peace Comes Dropping Slow *(Albernum Press)*
Tunnel Jumping *(Scarlet Leaf Press)*
The Blackstock Children *(Scarlet Leaf Press)*

A Wolf Rages Down the Little Jocko

by

Denis Stokes

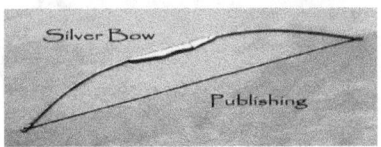

720 Sixth Street, Box # 5
New Westminster, BC
CANADA V3L 3C5

Title: A Wolf Rages Down the Little Jocko
Author: Denis Stokes
Cover Art: "Earth – Day 3" painting by Candice James
Layout and Editing: Candice James
ISBN 9781774033135 (Print)
ISBN 9781774033128 (Ebook
© 2024 Silver Bow Publishing

All rights reserved including the right to reproduce or translate this book or any portions thereof, in any form except for the use of short passages for review purposes, no part of this book may be reproduced, in part or in whole, or transmitted in any form or by any means, electronically or mechanically, including photocopying, recording, or any information or storage retrieval system without prior permission in writing from the publisher or a license from the Canadian Copyright Collective Agency (Access Copyright)

Library and Archives Canada Cataloguing in Publication

Title: A wolf rages down the Little Jocko / by Denis Stokes.
Names: Stokes, Denis, author.
Identifiers: Canadiana (print) 20240424182 | Canadiana (ebook) 20240424212 | ISBN 9781774033135
   (softcover) | ISBN 9781774033128 (Kindle)
Subjects: LCGFT: Poetry.
Classification: LCC PS8587.T64 W65 2024 | DDC C811/.54—dc23

**For Mary,
in wonder and gratitude,
for her courage and these journeys.**

A Wolf Rages Down the Little Jocko

Acknowledgements

Several of these poems have appeared in the following. Much, much thanks.

Grammateion; Queen's Quarterly; Quarry; Canadian Literature; Leaping Clear; Nebula; NuNow Anthology; Carrying the Branch (Glass Lyre Press); *Iowa Source; With Adam, Gathering* (chapbook, Albernum Press); Images Exhibition (Kennedy Gallery, North Bay ON); *Peace Comes Dropping Slow* (chapbook, Albernum Press); *Canoe Poems* (with Ian McCulloch, Bill Gibson and Laurie Kruk); *Cannery Row.*

The author is very grateful for Writers Reserve grants and a Works in Progress grant from the Ontario Arts Council. Much thanks for the gift of affirmation, freedom and time.

The author is most thankful for the warm welcome of the Malawi Teachers Union.

A Wolf Rages Down the Little Jocko

Table of Contents

I Plover / 11

Writing Something / 13
Jewels / 15
Plover / 17
Running / 18
Pakashgoogan / 19
Women Weeping at Kispiox / 21
Fudge and Coffee / 22
After Paganini / 25

II With Adam, Gathering / 27

Snowball / 29
Lake N. / 31
With Algonquins, Lac Clarion / 32
Ishpatina / 34
With Adam, Gathering / 35
Taché Revisited / 37
Driving / 38
Elephant Memory / 39
A Wolf Rages Down the Little Jocko / 40

III At Wasi Falls / 41

IV Crosslight, Baie Dorval / 47

V Tasting Africa / 55

Buying Balls Near a Rubber Forest Close to Nkhata Bay / 57
Tasting Africa / 58
Mancala / 60
Southern Cross / 62
For the Coffin makers / 63
A Poem for a Man Named Denis / 65
Pole Dancer, Bujagali Rapids / 68

North, eh? / 69

VI Postcards / 71

How Rain Arrives / 73
Tracking Winter / 74
The Table / 76
Deer Park - Zen/ 78
Deer Park / 79
Near Osprey Links / 81
Prayer of the Deer's Cry / 82
Portals / 83
Glimpses / 84
Postcards / 85
Safety / 87
In My Heart, Hong Kong, 1942 / 89
Quill / 90
Rear View / 92

Author Profile / 94

I

Plover

I am in love with this world.

~ John Burroughs

This is the present, at last. I can... This the now, this flickering, broken light, this air that the wind of the future presses down my throat, pumping me buoyant and giddy with praise.

~ Annie Dillard

A Wolf Rages Down the Little Jocko

Writing Something

At 4:30 A.M. I woke up
to drink coffee, eat homemade bread,
listen to Rampal play something while my eardrums
managed crazy arabesques in their dark
rehearsals, and look for a utensil

for ten minutes beside the lamp Grandma left,
sputtering its message of *wake, wake, wake* so I could
write something.

Now it's 7 A.M.
Rampal's achievements have gone the way
of the school marm in my clock's bell
and something is happening with light
beyond my window. I've done everything
but something we both might be ashamed of —
those humorous murders in the mirror.
Reader, I see your shadow there.

There's a duck a girl gave me
because I must have taught her something.
I've tried for half an hour; it's not quacked back.
Meanwhile, something can be heard
of the Canada's and grebe's return —
pre-echoes of my voice saying to my daughter,
"Look at the pond, Honey — they're here again."
She'll mutter something even wiser than my silence
then we'll both look away at something else.

I hear a wind picking up near my car wheels.
The itchy devils want to go. I've still not
written something, so I've been reading
how we are kites chasing a wind that gives us
something to chase with unmoved wills.
Now I am afraid: the sage writes,
make no vows, no promise to yourself
such as "Tomorrow, I'll wake at 4 or 4:30
and put something down on the empty page."

A Wolf Rages Down the Little Jocko

Also, God does not love fools,
even his own fools, the sage contends ...

I look down at my hands, twiddling ink stains
and this page, perfect with that silence,
full of nothing but an effort
to blank the wind out, tugging at a curtain
just a notch, tugging at some womb,
praying that something dreadful does not happen
to my car, Grandma's lamp, my hockey team.

Jewels

I can make what I want here, call this place
South Africa, a claustrophobic womb, wait patiently
for justice to suck me out into some glad nothingness
with no colour, no light left — the bruises gone
or unimportant. I can make whatever I want of
this sack, hurting my shoulders — it's too full of jewels.
They stuff my pockets so I can't move. Rubied wounds,
the hard blue mornings I was unable to handle,
the tiny green islands around my lady's finger.
It is all travel, rough work, back and forth to
old places until I rock, a child in a rattling cart
mining the ground, deeper, deeper into shifting
dust, day into day into — damned this swaying back.

An adolescent weakening reaches the knees, my shoulders
slanting badly away from this road. I keep turning
into myself as the jewels hide, as they cut me, then
shine. I wear the last light they gave. I wear
a slow smile, gentle and hardly there but for the jewels
that mark me. I sign their cheque book, read, 36%
Modern Poetry. I touch above my shoulder blade where
Gwen kissed. I feel the mark, a train's moon
that enlarges as it enters you. Goddamned the sway,
this little rest after the puppet dance, poor pay, hard
travel from each broken Eden. The road cuts my feet:
smithereens, scarlet marks of what my love can't carry.
Damned these fingers, dull, cumbersome, heavier and busier
about their braille. The jewels burn holes because
my fingers hanker so. My hands — seamless pockets,
dark and empty. I can barely hold them open as if I were
Nas-shig-y'alth, that bastard chief mining the darkness
while his tribe ate grubworms, his sack a dead weight of
light he'd taken. He could have healed their eyes into joy.

A Wolf Rages Down the Little Jocko

Raven, take me up again until I see the jewels that
make me: my father's eye that night, looking through me
until I couldn't sleep, my mother's mouth,
her tones of voice moving in me like blood,
fingertips of each woman who has touched my hand
with her hand, the amber hands of brothers, friends,
the black moon sliding across winter's glass,
my sister's first twirls in her 3-year-old yellow wool
and galoshes — these are all with me. Take them,
Raven, into the darkness which is my life. I wear
your ring, its seal beautiful as the wax sears.
Scatter the jewels, good black bird, wise and generous
trickster. I want them everywhere: young blue ones
of each night before, the red glimmerings of age,
the dwarfs I barely remember. Let them cut through
dark glass, this night that weighs down
with hard cold. Take me far through this
smoke-hole, closer. I must melt soon into my own
image. Make me all wings, a sudden falling.

Plover

I love how the spring air
hovers over the woods
after a light rain, brings
me to the plover,

  the wind carrying gold there
  in its wings. Its flight
  a silent soundwave, dips
  then lifts like
  Mary's songs.

  I love the plover,
  its colours of cold,
  snow on dark wood,
  cut wood, bold
  as ground flying.

Last spring,
all down the valley,
I called beside the water
to a new sky
I could not resist
as it listened
or did not listen:

I love the plover.

I love the plover.

Running

Half wild, this road
has lost its snow.
Only gravel and wet sand
feel my feet chained
to fartlecks, the heart's
commands of lefts and rights
through a cool evening blue.
Birds warn their mates of
a stranger through
gray vacancies of leaves.

A plover. Its laughter scatters
the path of air into sweeping water.
I'm soaked in mud but can't stop moving,
ankles creaking.
Yesterday, my car's choke
faltered over changing air.
Words run into ink the sky keeps releasing,
new water refusing to not move.

Near the birches and cedars
there, scuffles
leave bloodstains on young willows.
Why do I hurt so?
Ankles, knees, head,
chest heaving lungs
into hands around a knife, slicing
frost as it flowers?

Why is this hard on me —
returning to this running
over stones locked in shifting
clay? Where is this wind my body
chases? Some hot, glad animal
closes in.

Pakashgoogan

Some in the village
are calling your two sons
dumb Indians.

They say last night
was long in a cold
that can cut limbs loose.

In the ice crust
a moose could bleed
at the ankles, drop

on its path. It lasted
too long, George said. Beside
a one match fire

they slept in turns.
Around Trout Lake, birches
molt like beige snakes. Their skins

strike the fastest flames
in snow. In dreams,
the fire formed tongues,

their fast necessary.
Hares are scarce. Could visions
have come of arrows,

women, a name a song
for your youngest, half-poet perhaps,
midjis at 17,

his robin wine breast
bleeding out of a surrounding night
he refuses.

Midmorning, a wind
blasted from your rifle ends
from stars, his cry —

A Wolf Rages Down the Little Jocko

Pakashgoogan,
the stranded hunter's friend,
a ghost roaming darkening

snows, until good men
are found,
his rest in your relief.

Women Weeping at Kispiox

Their faces are the home posts cut from soft wood
Of cedar beams. Some red, some black lines barely hold
The rain back. There is the beaver clan and the frog clan,
The bear's family, the raven and all are sad.
The Skeena's a mean creek emptied from their veins until
The body becomes all water. Their time floats away.

I saw the conference at Kispiox. Chief Dan spoke
Of words. Hunters of guns while trappers defended
The conibear. The dance was glad but sad really
Like a last pow wow among clouds, then thunder
And no light. John Stanley spoke of plumbing in Stoney Creek:
Soon, these houses won't stand. All we'll have is our own

Survival. "Return, good bear" he prayed, "helping
Spirit. Trees, relieve us, shelter." The birds wouldn't defend
But there'll be berries, mushrooms. These women's faces
Soften with their own water. It's hard to know if they're suffering
Like demons or angels. Their daughter walks, man-less,
Out of town. Her feet toss sprays of tiny deaths behind her.

The sky balances its hoop dance. She sees the earth's egg.
She glimpses the raven's shoulders turning into wind.
The clouds shift onto the rockface over Trembleur Lake, sun-glint
Hurting, near Hazelton — the mantles of the Seven Sisters.
These totems, these few remains, weep themselves away. Rose,
What shall we do, old friend?-visit Tache, tell of K'san's

Ladders for the people, bright fevers reaching back
To health? We went to Kispiox, hoped for a few moments,
While Edgar got drunk, Darryl stoned at thirteen,
Louis, stabbed — a misunderstanding beside a cold stove,
Late winter. These women close in like night visions, weeping
Wood, faces veiled by faith saving beauty, red coat justice
Scouring mountains and Simon, last buck, rages himself away.

Fudge and Coffee

When today we skied the hills
would flatten us. *De fond*, au Quebec —
when in Rome. Across the dam, birches,
a convention's light demonstrations.

Olive and Roland
were finishing breakfast. Married
forty years, their cabin on the river
is a place for faces, stories told
of Algonquin friends here, the change
in children, of how the clouds
and animals move. We stumble
through joual our books can't master,
drink coffee and eat fudge, our skis
outside. Olive gives you the recipe.
You outline yours for granola.
Avec, Roland comments *"Bonne écriture."*
I steal some fudge
in a half-secret plastic bag
for Marc, back home, *keeping*
our precious child. No room in my vest for cardboard boxes.
Olive used a box eight days ago.

Grandmére used boxes too, her best fudge —
maple. Mom could never use
the recipe — either too soft or hard
or sweet, because of the oven. After
Grandma died, Mom never tried again.

In Prince George, we bought
our skis on sale, blowing our stipends
like pub money for wedding rings.
I'd come home after 50 tries, 49
unsuccessful, almost dangerous, entirely
comedy — that hill veering through
Fraser's ravine. Wrapped in brown
paper around a box, fudge and cookies
waited in my mail for me.

A Wolf Rages Down the Little Jocko

Mitts too, Grandma's design —
two-toned green. My aunt
sent them with a note. I can't recall
the words, though I cried
reading her scribbled prayer. I'd just
heard on the phone the night before
about her breakdown. How many
until then, I don't know. When
we buried her in Timmins, what —
the year we married, four hulking
brothers — we blubbered away...
John singing above the choir
How Great thou Art. They'd
been married like us — a couple of years.
Looking at my feet, I see a tear
on leather. I'm with her-'72, skipping

Chemistry. She tells me
walk on the outside, learn to
protect a woman. I sneak toys
out of her basket in the Chainways
store. She'd treat the whole world
to butterscotch sundaes, but no —
now, in that red booth, with her toes curling up, it's only me.

I think we should wax up our skis
again, those fast candles
full of the blue flame sky lights
on a cold day, visit
Olive and Roland for fudge and coffee,
get our Lara when we return, then
see Uncle John. The weather's
bad, but it's not that far
to Timmins. I could play darts
with him, down some beers.
We'd argue about the Maple Leafs.
I know, Honey, you hate
the thought of driving.
Since we slid into the ditch
last month, jolted end over end,

the north's no longer innocent for you.
the moon's a pirate's eye, night
a plank the sword winds push us along.

What people were with us
then, what angels, arms of God
that kept our child? Irish granny?
My grandad? A French Canadian
grandma who mastered arts of listening
while she'd cook fudge and steep the tea?
I sensed a man I've never met —
your father — if flesh is the only way
a person's known. Our trunk, full
of gifts for Christmas. That upturned
car containing presents too, my brave saint
had filled from her anxious winter basket,
these prayers I still can't understand.

After Paganini

I am thinking of the silence
music fills
around 1 A.M. when the day
arrives,
of the little knowledge
my ear holds, floating
with the folded airplanes of those
long dead—

a silence beginning
with Pachelbel in a moment
that the night almost held
still as borrowed smoke lifted
like a restless moth to a fixture,
a restless lover
kissing my wife's breasts good night,
listening to rustles from the crib
next door to us,
the tiny, frightened protests
of our daughter growing
what it takes to eat the world with...
A silence containing
in some way everything:
our walk up the hill in the first
spring light,
looking over the lake towards Val D'or
or eastward
where hills fall,
running into water, wild
through rock no-one's discovered,
then reaching
to the blue fires just beginning to burn
or the red flames
like our fathers' and mothers' faces
about to leave us, always here,
almost reaching through arms of the wood
holding all, including us...

The silence ended
with echoes of a kettle being filled,
a cup preparing itself
with my assistance
and in presences of steam,
ghosts lifting in one last noisy dance
to wake me
after a quick job on the cupboard doors

and another silence:

It is good to listen.
It is good to open the door
and take the air into us,
the last white stars of a hard season.

It is good to pray, listening to Paganini,
watching the only light in the room
and observe the dark, clouding Cassiopeia,
Betelgeuse, the faceless moon
that hurts and relieves.

It is very good to write this down.

II

With Adam, Gathering

Summering where herons stalk.
Wintering out among wolf-packs.
Plumed in twigs that green and fall.
What does he know, the man at the wall?

~ Seamus Heaney

and we have love and the god outside
until ice starts to limp
in brown hidden waterfalls

I am waiting for a new ship, so new
we will think the lush machine
an animal of God.

~ Michael Ondaatje

A Wolf Rages Down the Little Jocko

Snowball

At first, a white fluff
of summer, my daughter's rabbit
rolled in with mine,
timid with news of humans
but in their run, these sisters
would zip across the screen
like wild cursors or quick
exchanges in a chess game
pawn for pawn.

I see her twitching for knowledge
in our meadow's last autumn
clover, the fast skedaddle
at the sight of our border collie
crossed with sun's retriever,
chasing a white cloud of hunger
in longing to protect each rabbit
like fruit on a forbidden tree.

How the big sister
escaped in late winter,
giving up the hutch of love
they shared under stars
they could not see, remains
subject of speculation
even for my daughter's father
who buried it, wondering
of peels and potato eyes.

The younger kept breaking out
and kept returning in my
arms like the ghost of
a lover, growing larger
with each new absence until
I saw myself transfigured
one evening on the hill
after a late afternoon rain,

the June sun clearing
everything, the dew from
sky cool where Snowball
found cover in a copse
of low brush between two paths

but already she'd discovered
and mapped rocky releases
at the foot of her hill, holes
which could drive a dog mad,
make its master humbled, chasing
a rabbit he had just seen —
attempting to protect a cool ball
of life, rolling into a wild risk
my love, dangerous and wanting.

Lake N.

This evening, this sky is clear gift.
How my eyes in low light always lift.

The water waits, dark silver, smooth
to my hungry paddle as it scoops.
My heart floats in God's health.
My hands keep making cool cups
which hold my eye, my thirsting mouth
in each shrinking mirror, God's wealth

of what makes me and what's left.

With Algonquins, Lac Clarion

No moose horn then
calling our hunger
into battle, the lake's name
placed us between
Rapid Two, Sturgeon.

The pike cruised, slow
graceful submarines
boyhood dreams could
play, the reeds pliant
to the dance of water.

Then the stream deepened
into a pond widening
as if a field of barley.
In the pink light
I steadied the canoe.

On the first shot
the buck and mother
lifted heads to hear.
The second: the mother
lunged then turned to see her son

drop on one knee. Its gentle
genuflection troubled
the cow, their slow waltz
broken by a silence now
it could not comprehend.

The third blast chased
her away, water filling
the imprints of her life,
her offspring filling
our lives with time.

Into the fire, an offering
then rich smoke. I carried

A Wolf Rages Down the Little Jocko

that head over each portage
by its sprouting racks, velvet
and slipping, my fingers dropping

old songs and old demons-
devil tags, four by
fours, the old sudden
arrows- that eastern beer
I drank with a friend

close to an Atlantic
distance calling us,
his mom dead for two
weeks then, her comb
cold to his father's heel.

Ishpatina

For Ian

July again and that ridge waits,
its vision, falcon swift and mute,
mystic with lost tongues of earth.
Suffering under the hawk's nest —
Maple Mountain, nectar in bear caves
and everywhere we look, islands.

Each sky changing as we cross water
waves to a deeper Manitou, languages
of silent Mitsipishu, God's optic logic.
Light moves across our backs, before
our eyes, yet each stump and rock
shifts into blue gray manitous, moon hurts

deep enough in arms that reaching, throb.
Shores sense our legs then, but next?
We hollow out this emptiness, hands
carving lonely strokes, a crow's sculpture.
From our mountain, light catches
the last angles. It waits until this dark,

until we see it. In wives' eyes
there are places we are still left to climb.
Each time we set out, the ground moves.
Tenebres...quiverings...each unshot arrow scares
like mapless travel, heavy with dawn
each robin in us silent, wearing blood.

With Adam, Gathering

I walked early this morning, clouded
in early summer. It gave me dogs,
mosquitoes to clear the air, gave me
a cooling wind and hurt footsteps
carrying a wood scent, a memory
of rain, a broken promise in my
dream's flamencos, my busted love
nudging me back to an apple hunger.

...Shoving me back to an apple's
anger and the Lord watched me giving
in and the Lord keeps watching me
give new names to these old fevers
and everywhere was once garden here,
my instruments, my tools humbled
heavy on my shoulders, the fruits' stink
and shadow, heavy in my hands, my
touch — sliced by a sword of fire.

My sleep had been deep yet broken.
I hadn't played hockey for seven days.
No brew in the fridge, no sex. I dreamt
of a bear climbing a high pine, suffered into
an ugly woman. I downed my first draft again
with my cousin, on junk now. For Wicca,
a student touched her own warm earth. Dark

had fallen to its own music: Stones and
Zeppelin, Vivaldi weeping over leaves,
Mozart making sad rounds jig. Dogs yelped
beyond Bach's concerto of dreamed silence, spheres
moved, moving over a human deep. Our baby in arms,
I danced like a god, making, a moist woman, a coin's glint
in tiger light.

It was like this always: I would wake
to the knowledge of myself having woken —
a pickerel thrashing out his bladder's last air

A Wolf Rages Down the Little Jocko

on rocks at the Wasi — *here*. An osprey dropping
on Stormy Lake, near Commanda, its sudden sensing of
      talons down.

Nessie shifting under the loch's pibroch.

That someone was pleased for me—no doubt.
Light moved, large on a monarch's wing; once, we'd
made love in sand, on a shore while water
trembled, a path of web, glimmer. To make that day last.
By fires, I told my kids stories about the stars.

Yet there on Pine Lake, my son would stumble on that
rock's razing edge — cedar, rushes, fronds then
a drop into the darkest water. It was good
to swim there and land, to dry in the light.

Over the South River, we'd pluck buds and berries.
Maps in cloud shapes then, gilt edges, blood
and rose-light fading the blue wish of sky.

It's late morning, but it's still dark — this cave...
I snap fingers — magic: Grandma's lamp.

Now, a canoe on my shoulder, scratched green. I head to

an island,

      through mist   budging

                        brief
            a frog   undershadows,

                a
      Kingfisher's   wings.

Taché Revisited

That morning you came back to the cabin
and I'd made coffee and glad notes in a book,
the sky a chilly blue, an April stillness.
You swung two ducks through the door, your stride
a touch awkward because of the gun.
What were we thinking about, talking about-
each of us had found a woman we could love.

Walking across the rock, over damp moss,
we drank the spruce breath, though the cold
hurt our lungs because we knew that though
I'd made flames in the woodstove, the sun would soon
warm everything. We were anxious to discover
animals: bear and moose, a skunk or grouse,
but a black lab startled us, the way it hung.

Its dark absence still swings in me. Your wife's people
believed you were too dark for her to love.
Now softly, you carve out your heart in soft
wood, B.C. cedar far away. We talk of
fires, the same wood they burn, time's words,
smoke over surfaces of every lake we've loved,
of wood dreams, lost daughters, deaths which empty.

Driving

Southward and on the east rock
a bloodgold magic, birds
silenced by the fever in my wheels.
Miles gone yet at my shoulder
yours the feathered presence
of late light among these larches.

Elephant Memory

Mud in the pond's bottom or beyond
the river's edge, tusks attached to flesh
breaking down into a shining dark... Beasts
leave us: the captured snake you punished
because love mixed into another's fear, the dog
you loved honestly, imperfectly. These beasts
leave and in the wilderness, your rage almost
quietens and you return with woodsmoke and
the maple's shadow which is the half remembered
shadow of the baobab. You would be rogue
and mystic, contentious with a claim staked
on behalf of otherness, this impress on a woman's
skin she cannot imagine, will never remember.
These must be out of lifted trunks, water
everywhere. Beside our huts that night, a tree
knocked over like a grass blade in a big wind or that
afternoon, two villagers, nameless, I remember now.

Even the ranger, armed for dawn and distance
becomes anxious through under brush on this tufted hill,
watching the quiet in the fanning earflaps, draw
of hose and the suctions of green takings, columns
of an old building no wind but patient time knocks
down and we are blind men deconstructing ourselves
into a first word as though light breaks into river rush
or the violence and innocence of the Serengeti,
skills the wildebeest forgets, mastered briefly.

No camera could hold this — the silence behind
the image, this being here beyond silence
no lover could paint in trailing safety,
nor greed could poach out of shadows, nor
poverty kill out of deaths, cut out of
the fever tree. You will remember this deeply
as river mud shifting within you, ivory tired
into tooth, each key consumed by your own music,
this space all door and window, distance closing in.

A Wolf Rages Down the Little Jocko

This whitening winter which becomes your life
makes this frozen loneliness, crowding your blood

and if there were clouds intimating light
or some warmth to come, farther down the river...

You hear only days later in this nightmare
which holds you from the cabin in your heart,

all becomes a frost, cutting, a dark
charging you like an empty train with a dead light,

those eyes wild with the taste of your name
and with stripes which turn you into hard lines

of fear's prisoner. Its eyes widen to its leaps;
you squint because the sun is hard

with ice where you planted traps last week
and suddenly, you are not sure whether

you should run back to the highway's fever
or greet the beast, free at last, offering

your hand with all your life, your love.

III

At Wasi Falls

A Fishing Ditty

*...bottom feeders,
passing themselves off as leaders...*

~ Bruce Cockburn

And They Call it Democracy

A Wolf Rages Down the Little Jocko

At Wasi Falls

Here, I've come to love
the middle rock,
how the water
as it begins
to drop down
on its own knees can
move either way
under the tamarack's
shadows
and the birchlight.

How many times
has this lake
gathered my eye
into a gesture of
receiving grace until
all I want to hold
in my heart's counting
house was an old
economy which can only
give: that heron
priesting the south shore,
loon poised for its
breakdance just beyond
the ruffled surfaces
of love, that turtle where
the clear giving would
lap the pebbles.

How we saw — my son and I
fishing for some
deep secret here yet right
before us... In dewdrops,
quarrels...
is as it is,
was as it always was —
a sun's golden moment,
late summer.

A Wolf Rages Down the Little Jocko

    Late spring,
my wife and I would watch
the broken and glorious reaching of
pickerel here... Why do they
bother to bash
their own lives against
these rocks, as if
they'd read into the water's
whitening page of news
their own shelved life?

No salmon's gushing of
blood, in that sad drama only
the subtle inoculation
of the air's membrane
with a mere acquiescence
of death, that cul-de-sac
of impotence
and since it was
them, not us
our absence within their hot
suffering would leave us
emptied and chilled
while far off even as these
broken dancers spawned
a man's hand
in our city would sign us
over to fireworks
falling like sky over
this same lake...

    Queen Victoria —
smoking schoolhouse,
flashes, sputters of human light,
each sun exploding
like fading flames and glimmers
from a tarnished grail
and then the sick flickerings
of lost spotlights and garish stars,
a neon and violent

demonstration of light
dying like love in the heart's hospital.

Had we become
a people who loved
the dark nightmares of the poor
because those *fish*
drinking their own gasping lives
far down our same shore
would always
be with
themselves...
Here I struggled
with my visiting sister
to unhook a catfish
refusing to not live under
these cedars... the news
of lead leaders and barbs glancing
with the half-light
of another's dream —
ours.

      This mist rising
from Wasi Falls always
interests me, clears
my lungs with the cold
passion of dawn
as I edge along its descending
path, sometimes almost
slipping in, the view
too much gift at once at times
yet I want to hold
this ground, glad and unsatisfied,
lost, at home
with a God who watches us
like an osprey nested
on one of those dead trees
even if his game wardens, laid off
can't watch
and God knows

because he's just and sees well, I pray
even the odd bottom feeder
an accident in the nature of history
could spawn here —
this Bay lined with burnt bloodgold
that kind of muskie the tourists welcomed
from the deeper south
love as this moonlight must
somehow love
a kid grinding rice, gazing up from some
distant edge
some other shore, as this moonlight
wants to witness each penny of light drop here
a heart's bomb, on a lab's glass —
each drop of sick water half shining
yet in these minutes, rushing, counting down
could be a face, a candidate's chance
we'd come to love
in each dying moment we vote
for our best dying selves...

...could be as rich
with falling leaves of light
as these rocks centered
for this water dropping under
each minute's bridge even though
I hear goose steps
in my own heart, true —
my own goose heart's southbound
and golden moment
like any goose which could
as it must at times
fly south
into the codes of smiling signs
and an old remembering
to forget its own blessed place under these flaming
sumacs, in its own bird brain —
each candidate's
own cold Manchuria.

IV

Crosslight, Baie Dorval

To save a human life is as if one saved all humankind.

~ The Quran

I give you what you have already.

~ Juvenal

A Wolf Rages Down the Little Jocko

Crosslight, Baie Dorval*

1

And almost waking the dawn
I woke to the woods, crowing
their darkening shadows echoing
like frozen sonar over these heart
besieging snows and almost grateful
I wondered how today, craving
hearth warmth in courtyard,
marketplace, wincing as I glanced
goosesteps and the blue shirts
of a fear which keeps protecting me
while marching into April light
out of paths, our late winter sorrows
how would I yet again betray
myself, each torn page, each
split atom… How would eye's light,
each tenuous step a moment gives —
save, but for the back breaking
ledgers of my crushing failures
to love, pressed into an optic
fibre board of rut stuck walls
closing in, making within my heart
my own caveman's cave of
close called, far-flung shadows.
This was no time for prayer.

an outdoor Stations going through the woods close to Baie Dorval, Lac Kipawa, northern QC

2

And you are given, given, again
the crows cried. I could hear again
those dawns, August, Kashagawigamog-
their cries holding the sad, humorous
news that hurt has happened, keeps
hurting us again. Though
a robin, blood breast urgent with
ever reminding peace, three notes
always present in the half heard
spaces where we wait and wait
for each cricket to hesitate again,
this *midjis* sang out of silence, into
silence. I almost forgot the ides
arriving soon, the subtle thieves
of the crossed t's, actuaries
of a hell making somewhere
an off-shore paradise, or now
out of bombs carried on the backs
of children approaching crossroads
and trail ends, about to explode...
Jane, Finch, Malvern, Attawapiskat,
Baghdad, Afghanistan. I'd become
taxed too deep with tears. Now
outside, the intersections, changing
light. Within me, each new
lost path; surrounding me, these
dark woods. *And you are given
what you have already... had...*

3

Here were the unbearable pains
each other carried, way into way,
with which the crows woke me,
accused yet forgiven, my hand about to reach
for toast, a cup of soured water —
first breaking of the fast breaking
into day after a night of dreaming
like a goaltender clutching a goal back,
a miraculous save. Or lay ups
before the clock's sounding violence
which disallowed me, even as I dreamed
of bringing our cat's last days back,
flickering courage in his 8 lbs of
ego, I a butler sans master, monk
sans Pangur Ban, his mice — my words.
The crows knew this, nine-lived,
eight-fold rightness. I swear
I could taste their gladness.

4

Catching myself catching on
and on, out of this dying orange
light, these swamp green shallows
beneath this freezing thaw,
I would balance myself again,
again, clutch the ghosts of hope
in my spinal surgery's moon dance,
graced in the dark night of distant
bleeding glimmers and as buds
arrive and resurrecting, trampled
reeds, marvellous arrangements
of grasses, I would manage
step by trembling step, my uncle's
grass dance, from hand to hand,
the friendship dance as each friend
gathers into a sacred light of dying
or with these women, these garish
shadows, threatening, each part
of life, love which dries away,
their faces veiled by a strength
in beauty. I would pray into
a rain dance, wind sweeping
the unreachable plateaus, Nyika,
Zomba, Lake Malawi, while this
Galilee around which I live
cries out, two dusks ago out of
gunmetal shadows, blood-lined
light, for a traveller's trust, footsteps
over water. Will only our drowning
catch us? My friend, crossing late
April ice, cliffed into fall, sinking,
no boatman, Lord-saved to listen,
or Henry, clutching the gunwales
that morning we crossed Lough Derg.

5

Nets worked, in need of endless
mending, waiting as they dry
silently on rocks along each shore —
Don's salmon, Bray Head, Ontario,
Nipissing, we instead, over phone lines,
my mother, call across shadowed valleys,
forest paths beside water dropping
over stones, frog ponds, lakes,
kingfishers returning soon, catching
blue fire, or hawk wings crossing each
field of light, and moved into morning
I would find the lost ones here, that couple
like shadows plumbing a pipeline to
the bottom of Trout Lake, or Sarah-
her body at the foot of some weak tree,
no tracks on that path behind Northgate...
that unsteady hiker, gone years now
or that young Luke my son's age
gone into the hard-fought dark,
barring a safe step into streetlight,
his name crying out of ground for some
healing story. I would gather them too,
my mother, your hen's love, these
fragile chicks under these shattered
plinths, crumbling temples, crushed
between walls, this darkness of our cities.

6

Before that partridge last week
left no image but a silence at
the trail's end... Before screwing on
the whitewashed doors of our cups'
and plates' sepulchre, I nail up
a picture which might be a universe —
fires of falling bodies, multi-coloured
spheres, faces of some aliens, distanced
with a warmth which might befriend, or
was this, in the other frame, cabin imaged
into wood as though my own heart, only
chunks of stars, shards of our mirror always
about to shatter into coins about to shine
in some dump or gutter, or catching early
light, only gold spraying out of the mess
and straw of some scarecrow, his stilled
grass dance, this hill field soon lined
with the blood moon and the crow's silence?

V
Tasting Africa

**A hard road.
The one who has arrived has a long way to go.**

~ Tomas Transtromer

From '*An African Diary*'

A Wolf Rages Down the Little Jocko

Buying Balls at A Rubber Forest Close to Nkhata Bay

1

String-crossed, star-crossed, some are the sun.
Some a moon and others, earth, venus, mars.
These boys, straight as trees, see us and run
until the car stops. They play hard at these wars.

Each ball's dropped, springs up as if alive
from hard ground. Each hand presents a world —
Kwachas half haggled, begged. They could live,
if lucky, for days if one ball's sold.

2

You let this fellow claim a deal
twenty kwachas past the price you clutch.
Legs undercut, he'll whine then wheel
another sale at your expense. Our driver hits the clutch.

3

Windows rolling up, now these boys recede
into a world soundless with bouncing space,
these trees reaching into monkeyed sky, wind freed
of dreams. Behind us, our rubber leaves no trace.

Tasting Africa

I am tasting Africa — Yergacheffe in this café,
this young woman's eyes, silver, a skin all pearl
and her hair a brown river through a wilderness
of dream. I am tasting Africa with this scone,
listening to a speech I read at fifteen for no particular
reason — Haile Selasse. The coffee is deep, rich and dark
but a touch dry on the surface.
I lift my cup as one might lift the weight of slaves.

I am tasting Africa, Mzuzu of the highlands, orphans
clapping in the backstreets of Ekwendeni, the ground rooted
expanse of wind across the Nyika of swift-footedness
and the graced canopies of brachystegia. I am tasting
the kiln fires of Dedza, the bittersweet chalk of the technical college
in Lilongwe, the blue of Cape Maclear like a kid's freezie,
bright deep blue from Livingstonia to the Chipome Valley
as I gaze back, below- throat gulping at the Lake of Stars.
I am tasting Africa, Harry's Bar, Carlsberg, Carlsberg,
Huche Kuche and goat's head and roast chicken, meals
prepared by Tami — sheer selfless, self-filling art,
the blood of Chilembwe and the marble dust at the monument
of Hastings Kamuuzu Banda, on the way to the airport
along the winter dry Kamuzu Road. I am tasting
the dew I was then, as visitor, perhaps friend and in the dewdrops,
quarrels. I am almost tasting the mvuu farting, assured
in pure presence: *this is my territo*ry, crocodiles, fish hawks
all quarter and respect... Shire River of ghosts and bones.

I am tasting Africa and I have stopped dreaming:
no Kim Bassinger or Meryl Streep waiting beside
some dangerous Serengeti, no Peck or Jaluka waiting
on the peaks of Kilimanjaro crying out 'sing your song'.
I am singing of Africa, the song in my ear an unsung song.
I am tasting Kenyan coffee, *President's Choice*, purchased
unlike, I confess, my normal OFT...praying to Kenyatta —
a name muttered with reverence by Father Quinn once, petty
and effeminate, as he wept openly before us,
having returned '71, from Biafra... They cry, they cry:

A Wolf Rages Down the Little Jocko

the heart's dark in London, the darkening heart
of Ottawa, Antwerp, Amsterdam and Washington —
the beloved countries of lost tribal lines and fires...
Bantu, Chichewa, Tonga, Ngoni. I am tasting Africa, pray
to Dallaire and to my friend, once a Shell corporation lawyer, half
saint now, one with nature, whom I forgive as I read
Soyinka, Walcott looking back in hunger, Arthur Nortje
blown out like a quick match in a damp wind, the water jars
borne like dreams of children carried by graceful, draped women.
I am tasting Africa, remembering Nairobi six months ago,
the drying streams near the gaping silos, the carvings sold
in the airport — half Indiana Jones, half Bogart, the bottled
water, coffee beyond description, the carved giraffes and
cold Tusker under low ceilings. I am tasting Africa and it is
good — bloodroot, red bush, high ground, patient wind,
the sun above diamond glint in the crow's eyes — hard and long.

Mancala

Sun washed, polished by wind, wind's water,
these stones must be child-gathered by the lake.
In your fingers, each roll's a fingertip's gift
into a tiny bowl in a small tray of wood.
The table's graced with a time that space shares,
each hand reaching out like a star, alone.

With an anxious fever, you scoop each stone
by stone, then drop them into the next pool of water.
You're a god gathering all planets and stars
caught in a billiard run of sink, give, take
as though these stones were eucharist and food.
You pick up what the gatherer before has left.

A tiny cage for birds, your cupped hand can sift
the air and the air's song, like breath through bone.
Each pebble drops like a penny. The game's understood.
Your speed picks up wind like a growing daughter
moving along a shore of angels, castles, rakes.
You are moving the stones along like market wares.

On carefree days, friends, these the only cares:
to scrape out these valleys, pretend to fill the rift.
We will play soon, brothers, for higher stakes.
Sisters, what will fill these furrows when seeds are gone
beyond the sun's dance moving the dancing matter?
'We have done everything we thought we could.'

They will do everything someone hoped they should.
The sky will bleed out water, stones dropping with flares
lighting each face leaning down to find a better
stone as another hand grabs the ground we'd lift —
this earth pressed by fever into blood and stone.
Our hands move along table land until the fever breaks.

Stones gather like lover's eyes, stars above this lake.
I can tell by your faces that this game is good,
even if a chance is dropped, a decision blown —

each moment, a fevered reed along these windblown shores...
This game allows each hand to share in the theft
of what counts, fingers climbing a horizontal ladder.

You clear the wooden tray. Each friend can share
turns beside the lake as though exchanging gifts.
It's all one table: *Huche Kuche*, bottled water.

Southern Cross

Half truck, this land rover takes us through dusk into dusk of a light surrendering to the animals' secrets, low bushes arranging borders of a random path our wheels take, slowing over a sudden culvert a brook's established and as the engine's gunned, jolting us towards an upgrade, we sense something falling and it might be the dark.

Now the violent and wondrous beams of a searchlight, refuses to scan sky, only pot shots and double takes there, a small herd of impalas, striped light on the brown furred earth they carry, hold in their stillness; now a mongoose — did you see it... there's another then the light shifts to our passenger shutterspeeds and pauses, lost now for an invisible, snake-less ground. Now here's a bush buck close to the fever tree and that baobab and look — in the low cover of grass — a nightjar... and later, hippos, crocodiles, gentle with the river.

Tomorrow, we wake before six and with this man, we'll walk a mile or so behind his shoes, crouch low behind an eight-foot anthill, an elephant feeding on peace at the river's edge, the air cool enough to register his frost breath, dust breath and I notice this man with the rifle whom god has named Danger, tense until our silence becomes palpable so our safety keeps his job. Over coffee, he borrows the lodge laptop, answering my questions with images of orphans his wife is watching now, close to Ilongwe. The building they line up in front of is as a simple as a secret.

Now, the darkness is absolute as the possibility of justice and God. The rover parked, the search beams off, we are lost in a solitude that wells into this vast expanse of diamond-like glowing then end-stops in a cave's page. It makes us float, these stars, closing in on us as our eyes reach away. Above us some of the old stories, old hunters come, but this is no sky I've known; here, no old silence. Where could we be landed? Here as on Brobdingnag? Starships or some voyageur canoe... Look, look — this spangling mess of stardust, visitors' dew light, points joined... *The Southern Cross.*

For the Coffin-makers

In the dry season
there will be no worry
of wood rot, your wares

crafted and displayed
beside the red bricked projects
in the prosaic light of day.

This is the dry season.
As if facts will matter.
This Carlsberg truck could be

a Bedford box on wheels, glass
bones rattling us into garrulousness
and silence. Your furniture is rich

with a plush shining, no glut
of privilege here, no oystered
irritations, only the crass glory

of your craft — laminations, a little
veneer of Mzuzu pinings and these
boxes almost oblonged for shoulders

and belonging while these years, your
work picks up
like the Ilala Ferry crossing no lake

but this the forgetting river, its lights
blood red, its vessel's skin half
torn as the shirts, dresses of orphans

of Lilongwe, Ekwendeni, Itatu,
a vast grandmothering of earth even as
this earth leaves us praying for

no rain god, no propitiation
in the night fires cleansing earth of
hunger, fear, facts of life

A Wolf Rages Down the Little Jocko

and death which becomes life's
story. In the last light in the eyes
of your children, in this market's place —

this work of your hands.

Poem for a Man Named Denis

With the wind howling like the dogs of Lilongwe,
an early snow having laced my windshield
near this late November of tumbling flowers
I must lament for Shakespeare, choking
at my age on pickled fish and tumbling ale,
his life all too brief, his endlessly humbling
search for women and heroes while I'm left
singing of the same winding search. Even
though I've stayed amazed at my old friends'
singing, their faithfulness to the glorious
inadequate way of words as Will was
and some he loved — big hearted, big time
Ben and somewhere in the lull of touch
and prayer, unseen, unheard John Donne,
battering the walls, heart battered in God.

No, I am fifty-two and though not dead
yet, I sing that even now I have found a new hero
and but for geography, largesse and always
his casual integrity, not too Christly out of
reach and thus seeing, in my own face perhaps
a dark chance of a dim glimmer. It's not just
the large arms and heart with which he fills
a shirt, the glad badges of friends from South
Africa, it is the sweep and reach of each moment's
stride into more life until even his noise becomes
a prayer of spiritual strength for spiritual strength.
On Safari, before the perfect silences of the lost
Hunter, the Southern Cross, he waves at hippos
and thinks he might intimidate a grouchy,
munching elephant two hundred yards away or waving
later from the boat at fish eagles, half content
in their trees. He won't let me sleep under
those same stars in a tent resembling Escort or
North Face, but leaves me in a chalet so that
half drunk, I might sleep through a rogue's
rampage at the tree between us, a day after
two villagers across the Shire have under

elephant feet, met their maker. His cell phone
all beep and flash and percussion, all counter
point and reference, becomes a holy toy of talk, kibitz
and love, each recent encounter folded in with
the sudden ceremony of a welcoming party until
the name he announces becomes my name because
it is my name but not my name but the way
a name might be called by some hero beyond
and close to you as in another nature park
he calls 'Come and see this', while a large snake sleeps.

Fish broken on the shores of the lake, bread
broken and light arrives across the bay, and you see
a face, the woman who's made the fire not half
loved enough but a joy lives in the chair, on
the table and the tiny, roofed rooms at each end
of a shore's path, Nkhata Bay, Lake Malawi.

And if my friend did drink, I would sit with him
again, because God will give us friends, not just
heroes. I would confess that I too share a dangerous
amazement at women, how blessed and difficult I believe
our wives make our lives until something other
than growth cannot be an option. I'd talk with him
perhaps of his Presbyterian ministering father, of the human
mysteries of a love which hopes in a human sky,
of Iona, Livingstonia and George McLeod.
                                        Here,
I'm enjoying recalling how in the presence of an intelligent,
perhaps benevolent official with the voices
of a new nation, an ancient people, stammering
in the frozen numbness of fear, echoing with unheard swish
of slaves in the river, the ascent and descent, for
protesters, a language of crocodiles, each muddy silencing:
'I have no fear in saying... I have no fear...'

Without fear or much hope for myself I'll try to move
out into my cold and tree clinging dark today,
somehow more noble that I've found a new hero
at such a ripe age, that because he's become not just

A Wolf Rages Down the Little Jocko

a friend, but even a loved brother without the same
last name, I must end this now lest his large presence
distract and impose even as his head could swell
so I might hug my young daughter, so I might imagine
you, Denis, camping in Algonquin Park, my revenge
stamped with rutting moose or sweet with blueberries,
tumbling and outside your tent, a large bear.

Pole Dancer, Bujagali Rapids

For Chris Karahunga

Gnarled carving come alive out of tree,
into, with each blooming moment, a tree's
reaching as he roots himself and sky
turning, leaves, this is Quasimodo beside
these waters rushing within the darkness, sun
above, buzzard hard. This is a twisted Christ
twisting on his stick, his dance heavy
with the gymnastics of silence, this river
becoming the muffled echoes of Amin's screams
and the old dreams of Soyinka, Kenyatta,
the work carried once by the Shire away
from Livingstone, now merely ghost blood
over the lake, the Arab traders near
Nkhotakota long gone as the memory of
tribes and old betrayals. 'He is making
something of himself', the Bujagali Rapids
dancing to his dancing on his wooden leg.
He is dervish and drunken leprechaun,
this pot gathering with coins covering eyes
of the recent dead, now balanced beyond
himself, right arm a leverage against the...
certainty of a fall. Now he half somersaults,
car wheeling wagon, some ghost horse
following. Now he leaps on some invisible
bungee of ancestors gods might save
before the impact with a patient ground.
The cheers come as though an angel's thunder.
We grow tiredly amused, look out at water,
almost ashamed here as his dance gathers
wind and a stamina's grasp, wondering what
could we do, a veil torn here, all cathedral
as we glimpse this impossible man not man?
What would we, will we ever do? Here? Now.

North, eh?

How often, is it, do you eat hippo meat
and when elephants rage, do your houses
hold and what is that red leaf in your white
sky ? You mean even your electric defuses
too — wind, snow... You can walk, like Jesus
on lakes, then auger water with a sharp stick, right
to the bottomless centre of a frozen 'night night' story,
'til no cichlids come? But 'chub' shines, freezes

the turning chambo onto a winter's heated table,
your shacks the size of our shacks? But we live
in ours, our sticks for cooking; you have no Bible
knowledge, isn't it? Yet Noah would leave
moose like an ugly waterbuck, the busy beaver
eating mountain trees near Mzuzu. You fib well!

A Wolf Rages Down the Little Jocko

VI Postcards

It will talk as long as it wants, this rain.

~ Thomas Merton

     **in the blue night
first haze, the sky glow
with the moon
pine treetops
bend snow blue, fade
into sky, frost, starlight
the creak of boots.
rabbit tracks, deer tracks
what do we know**

~ Gary Snyder

**The year before I die, I shall send out four hymns
          to track down God.
But it begins here.
A song about that which is near.**

~ Tomas Transtromer

A Wolf Rages Down the Little Jocko

How Rain Arrives

Maybe the postman
is a drunken hunter
eating up the road for dogs
with his four by four

and his wife waits
for his letters, crying
above North Hill, high
through a tree we can't see

or God teases blue
asters with wet stars, alone
in their unities of
falling, or

this is just a gift-storm
we're hard-pressed with
buckets for, how rain
arrives is

a problem for
a person with a big black
flattened hat, ready to
dry his eyes out.

Tracking Winter

After rain and thaw, the cold comes back.
A hard wind. Then settles into wet, almost
light frosting snow, gathering on roads, that soon
the fir trees wear. On our lane, ruts deepen.

At the top of the hill's crest, the inlet slush,
soon solid, wolf tracks which with a later
page, I will confirm (redundantly) or fail to confirm.

Crying out in the early morning for service
our cat's left, with the dogs, this tracking literature
of movement beyond the house, silent, soon
covered with a deeper silence which I prefer.

Just before the first snow a week ago, a severed
deer's hoof, fur soft, thin and nut brown, shit
brown, close to its bone. A few yards away,
its face beside the rest of itself, snow tailed
and gut light eviscerate, keeps watching
for wolves, fire clad, teeth whistling through air.

First rabbit tracks, gathered footings before each
leap, each little fore foot reaching beyond itself,
hind muscle explodes, following the ear twitching
with the hurt for joy, low spruce or biting fear.

I trudge, tracks half shadowed, dragging this sled, heavy
with wood once, once again with half frozen beer,
soup cans, a book, over hills rolling with laughter,
someone's tires of a four by four, firmly pressed into
the road's skin, cooperative with the weight of power.

As the ice keeps hardening, the snow covers, beneath itself
its own depths, under the old, frosted window, this pipe
from the sump pump keeps clinking into slush
and spray, concrete relief, the ground's river song.

A Wolf Rages Down the Little Jocko

No tracks found yet of a chickadee flitting
twig to twig, its battery of a tiny radio rasping
peaceful and urgent static, nor of the blue blade
of sky slicing air in a jay's wing, green tree to
green tree. Nor the crow's wing, the raven's hooked
gaze, pine high over low cast shadows — I can't
be looking. I cannot be looking. Or no food.

In the moistening mud close to swamp beneath
a slight ridge (gneiss or 'royalite' ?!), large tracks, still
clawing at autumn in soft stump wood and later,
a steaming seat, jazz rising through no blues now —
final wandering steps, before sleep, among last things.

I could never stop loving this path, cut from
outcrops, set straight by some invisible arrow.
Overlooking, it traces the Wasi, old tracks
of ghost trains, ghostly beneath my boot prints,
each snowdust from hemlock in a wind's breath,
nudging life into me and outwards, nudging love.

      Lake Nipissing/Lac Tee/
      Lac Temiscaming/Wasi River

The Table

The white table was freezing movement, with nicks from heavy dishes or a kid's fork, missing. My son's plate was still half filled, the macaroni glowing with orange light, his blood's half hunger. His voice lifted from the basement with my daughter's voice, each drawing lines around and between themselves as furniture dragged skate marks into the carpet. They were making a place, playing house and the sharp insistences of who would be who (how) warmed the stairs with their names, their love, their distance. To the left, the fruit leaped at the eye, taking up space, that odd third dimension (If I reached them, there might be something I could hold or eat until the apple would be in my brain, the banana that still wore the sun's mark from a place Gaugin had visited until he became... changed — one wife and daughter somewhere else — the banana would reach loins and that soft soil, that bog, would grow sore with pressure and potassium, the peach might carve its own poisoned stone from my heart.) It is to identify them as aflame and there, like the cloud that last night, hung beneath a full moon in a clear dark, all late September stars. Its edge curved, widening in all directions at once. It is to say they were planets in some half fated or providential, serendipitous reunion for my tired eyes. The dessert bowls were not cupped hands of angels, but the rice was soft, milky and sweet. The knives weren't pirate swords, the forks not pitchforks, but how did they fall there on the table with that absent magic of having a job done, laying angles imagined in the Pythagoras or deaf Beethoven in God's thought? What was the plant thinking — suddenly arrived in a red basket because of a sale? Its tag said four dollars; its green leaves seemed dervish mad with reaching for life. Under the woollen lightshade, the air moved in a jazz dance, in passionate detachment that must have held dust from my own breathing, my own dying skin. Each object located itself precisely with random joy, entropic surrender, indifferently aware of the other, sparks flying invisibly yet heard in my own heart's slow heat — its blind dog vision, until I became the bowl in the hand of a desperate grateful beggar, catching a coin from a friend in Algiers or on that street in Dublin. Our baby was cooing in her room a language she'd not yet forgotten, interspersed with calls of Da Da Da (filling her diaper), while from woods behind us, jays were taking blue wafers from the sky and bringing them to nests in dwarfed cedars. Soon partridges would fly off the handles of their own drumming ground, while echoing, our hearts would catch other distances, a human thunder.

Deer Park

Zen

While reading Osip Mandelstam in that library
where, years ago I first learned to read, a printout
pops out of the pages. Four books taken,
the place Deer Park, a theme I've prayed
for almost a year now: Gautama's fires, the Wasi
wild with antlers and white tails, last week's
collision, then that place, where, visiting, I walk
often, just north of St. Clair, the ravine
dark as any waiting for light while everywhere
culture crashes down, then the dogs come,
the women, the men in love. I wonder
who is this who would read what I
would read. I imagine a woman, lonely
for the god within that might heal each
of us, the holy broken witnesses,
their prophetic silences gracing into tale,
song... Franz Kafka catching the castle's
trying twilight, some final glimmer falling
like a benevolent judgement from above,
the moment's pogrom laughing into the face
of the Baal Shem Tov. Now, I must get back there
again to Laurence, the homeless friend I've met —
each possibility within the darkness of our
pockets. He might know: who is this friend,
silent across this Siberian page of deepening self
so true that the soul's inflamed and enraged by
these agendas of blood and lies, or this woman
perhaps- too beautiful and distant to love,
but would read this, weeping, and receive.

Deer Park

-1-

Here, at first
I thirsted
for the deer's run
a direction
to the stream's
whispering dream
of clearer blood —
a water's god.

Or was the thirst itself
the stream of self
chasing its own hot fever
beyond reason and an endless forever
of not this, not that
the gut's knot
in the scrabbled earth
of worldless worth

in the deer's own cry
which was my cry
and hunting with
the deer, caught word of death
stretching neck, soul
away from the hunter's thrill,
the blood run, the gasp and cold
stillness of the tree's bone, wild

life in the stag's branching head,
a freedom which led me
to this hunt
for that woman's kiss
beside the deer's stream,
this hunt from dream
into dream, under the frozen starlight,
once a young lover kissing his young lover goodnight.

-2-

Here, all's a deer park
the rising dark
of October mist lifting
from reed and stream, theft
of this heaven
falling on no deaf ears, this old news of living
in a heavy, flying joy
this day into day.

So, for a song's spring
or a lush green twig
I keep wandering, the water's song
always echoing
while this fire within my head
and the belly's flames would
draw the wind to me
as if it's only wind I see —

in a wilderness of mirrors
a hungry coupling of mirrors
begetting mirrors
mirroring more and more…

this and this, that, that.

Near Osprey Links

Osprey eggs legislated into golf balls,
these slopes shaved green, glowing with
a teletubbies discourse, a comfort beyond
the telling, the path to cranberries and cold feet

warm and easy now, as landscaped as any
Southern Ontario reserve; at the turn
I almost catch it again- deer shadow, much
darker than the sidelined car, gunmetal gray.

My daughter, beyond weeping, in the back seat,
my wife's friend a spiritual master when
she sings a psalm, flicks on the wiper blade
upon the impact of buck on windshield,

and later waiting to meet them at her house,
I realize, turning back towards the scene, I know
those strangers, stopped by a running shadow
until much later, some white winter hart

arrives with the live ones at the Shannondale
Field beside my other daughter's school, leaving
just a pub's name in some Wessex tale I drink
in, dreaming Hardy dreaming sheep in skies — child

again, amazed, upturned, gazing through cattle legs.

Prayer of the Deer's Cry

...or that as passing deer, like Patrick
these might, unseen, flee safely through
these woods, Lord, beyond the drying fields — that child
half clothed within the spider's web of screen frame, or each woman
facing the fire and rage behind the rapist's eyes.

Patrick, bind whatever Christ there's left
weaving through these bloodstreams of light
within this world, Word unheard?... shining
invisibly out of eyes, still, leaves wearing no
hankering light to turn over to the bloody fingered
kings, each dead stone closing over each dead thing.

Portals

October ending and this mild night
milky with sprays of flowering stars,
my daughter, twelve with fevers cutting
short her costume time: at the entrance
of a portable garage easy candy's disturbed
by an uneasy welcome, the host reaper's mask,
meeting screams and long gown running, ghostly into
lamplight and her shadowed father at the road.

That I would sense my dead — father, friends,
appears a trick dreamed out of prayer
with them — amazed, continuous sense
them more these moments than any other moment
as if entering your lover in dark joy
opens into love or love's dream beyond release —

tentative, sudden with unexpected hope-
unseen, felt, sensed. That I would
sense you my dead as if you don't still live
in me, beyond the muttered or discovered words,
beyond what I loved in you, remembering now
at this moment, my love, isn't it, autumn winding

down soon into paths, leavings, air carrying
the ghosts of leaves as our daughters at
their doors, our son's voice warming the phone
beyond our reach, within our faith in him,
hope for them... your departed brother slipping
pound notes into my hand to buy a round, or
across this road, six deer crossing, woods to woods.

Glimpses

Where that path branches after the high rock,
mossed, up from the pond of geese, each beaver's stick

I think I've caught the plastic back of an old chair.
Instead, the fawn's ribs given to the wolves' care.

* * *

.

Postcards

Arrangements, unanswered letters?
They hold their place well, in perpetual transit
from open drawers. Each duck and sunset, unholy flowers
crave a word I might send a friend.

Flying down Highway 11, my daughter flips open
her frozen meat box of cards with care, explains
to her Granny from Ireland "I like collecting them"
then presents like a last graduation of dreams
each occasion's place, name. Later,
I tuck her in with a book, a song on tape,
a prayer for all these people in her cards.

8:45:
Her brother's pink covers, soft wool, the stuffed rooster
which wakes him early, the horse which carries him away
or the silo on Grandma's rug, heavy with the harvest of play —

These can't handle him. A strange room, his grandparents' bed.
The dark falls to shapes, threatens him.
His usual room with Granny there. I'm "beside" feigning
sleep, my face wet with hot kisses as a truck
wheels over my nose until I'm gone to the place of parents
falling to example. Close calls, bills enlarging into monsters...
old friends nagging for cards and letters.
Sleep's conspiracies make me hide
like the friar with the same haircut my wife has snipped
onto my son, heroic robbers who've owned these wilds, hidden

from death. First, I try to tuck the news away —
Cambodia, steps exploding, people drifting like ghosts
from their own hunger — one woman still
beautiful, perhaps quiet, her small son
with soft hockey tape for his burns, his face
full of angry questions and I cut this card out
like last night, Ken's paper tuxedo, tuck it away
in my own dark places, carry the boy,
his mother, the stick man hooked up to western luck

A Wolf Rages Down the Little Jocko

and intravenous. I walk with the postcard until
it grows unkempt, heavy, until I must finally cut something
out of me, or write, or fly myself into hard travel.

A Wolf Rages Down the Little Jocko

Safety
-Tiananmen

So this, love, like that Hong Kong Alley.
Behind us, the fallen lives of all our friends——,
ahead, the snowflakes of Minshan that
Mao praised, once the dragon's flames.
They are calling us the children of the dragon,
not wild ducks calling across this darkness
of moving borders. Ahead, my love,
the darkness of moving borders.
By the time this comes, you will have found
Xinjiang. Through the underbrush, Li,
tell my people I am still happy. Tell
of our passion, our little fire I guard
within my teaching heart, how it will not will
itself away, swept by the widening fires
of truth in our love.
                        I have made it through
the valley. At first, some monks kept us.
We craved safety. A while now, am I
that girl to you in Tai's Alley? I wear
her sadness like a clove flower. Now,
they say the west is moving in, their phones
and cameras. If you see Kuan,
let him know my heart holds no coldness —
When the soldiers tramped beside my cell
(My face hidden by an old man's beard!),
I knew how the taste of fear can teach betrayal.
Now the others wait for words. Do they know yet
the tanks that chased us down, mangled Chen
and left us for paper dolls in hate's hard wind,
that they have invaded the people's hearts?
The people escape from their own freedom.
In your eyes, Li, my unborn children,
though between us, one vastness is all we see.
They will not know our new leader.
Her suffering will make her strength beautiful.
But I will not drift away, a soft blurring dream...
I am staying now with Sun's family. I look

like the child I was once. I gaze, ponder
past, future, the samurai sharpening in my heart.
I gaze at moonlight, grinding rice, at sunlight
in the dampening paddies, stooping, my face
shines in the glowing mist.
                                You?
You were called the rooster, crowing light
into each weakening betrayal. You will be
My homing bird and though you will be tired,
your wings will carry, love, the blood and light,
the unbearable weight of each setting sun.

I am looking out still… This water gives no answer.
When you find me, the red dress over the
white — how my loveliness will enchant you.
We will have passed those heartless willows beside
the sergeant's wall. We've sung our speeches, spoken
songs and somehow these words will echo into light
on young faces. They will carry their own
alchemist's burdens — fool's gold
of false care, half-lit shadows racing
over their half-dying flames. If life is but
a smile on the face of death, I smile for you,
my love… Search… seek. In that false spring
how could we rest? Sometimes I hear
the east wind moan in me like last gasps
from our red candle, then the thought's,
His dragons, knitted, deep in God's weaving fire,
which knits again, purls, as above my
nipple — your thumb. Unspun? You will gather
my fragrance in our dream, take my pink,
thin hand. Our love for them will keep.
I wait by watered embers, wearing your gift of
that hairpin phoenix, in that storm, Franklin's key.

In My Heart, Hong Kong, 1942

For Bryce Craig

For the past two days
I have witnessed the life
of prisoners, their war
humorous until... Until...

Now everywhere I look,
I'm clubbed by foreign orders.
Fate has become a wind
beating me into a shadow.

I am working in a mine
near North Point. I am only
weight and dust. Welding
in a shipyard, I help enemy vessels

head off to sea. I see feet dangle
above sharpening shards. Salt
is shoved carefully into each wound.
I am waiting for death with strangers.

Quill

Its edges roughed up,
its dun beige stripes
seeping earth brown into
a darker spine almost
a foot long bending
like a divining twig,
this eagle feather once
carried meat to crags
over Trembleur Lake
a flight no longer seen but
for the dance and filigree
in this shape of life's
shadow, a gift for
strength from Florence
Sam to hover over each
threshold wherein my
hunting might grow
humble enough to know
the flight that reaches
into the endless ceremony
of surprising otherness
high over water, high,
landing onto ground.

Domano, Thunderbird...
I would keep wreathing
my own holy word
carved out of hardening
pine with this wingborne
hope, tired now as I
think of it- my un-compassed
dislocations love's water and
life's clay flying in freefall
light through these soft
taloned fingers, holding
the hunger bravely
and carrying fear
to a nest I trust, my

children enlarging my
heart even as they
gorge on a lifetime's
entrails that sweeten
with memory I know,
even as a ghost
I embrace in a dark
where an eagle's eye
is useless but for
the mapping of rockface
and shoreline, opening
fields wherein, my father,
we plant what we
can't give and take away
with us what others
won't consume, even
this ground broken for
some unknown growing
into seed rising into bread
I'd break again if
I could, Dad, if I
could and is it light
I hear moving into places
where your voice, full
with a word, falls
into this feather still
softening silence, so
heavy to hold... If I
could only hold it, you,
my father but instead kiss
this feather as if it's all
you've become. And more.

Rear View

It's maddening, to catch these faces
half familiar in darkening twilight

of moving windows, these headlit moons

always almost about to arrive
like one last offer of your lost lover's breast

your fever close though distant —

this milky expressway of exits/entrances,
green signs heavy with the white names

of travel, each one a step, a kind

of home. You press the pedal
anxiously, these white eyes of strangers

wearing red traces of quick stops, quick

silver lifts out of this night's cold flow
and you see your brother-he's winding up —

a knuckleball. You see your old skates

glinting, your father cleaning the basement
in a rage, that house sold for over two years

and you see your sister as someone else —

she acts that well. Your mother's at a camp
for poor kids, her stories — low horns

waking you out of a summer's yawn

and you see the books, Christ, written
by writers, and the lovers, how they typed

glad brief poems all over your skin.

Each face you leave makes your darkness
precise, each round light a eucharist

melting to the tongue's gratitude.

Now your hand clutches vacant space, hugs
an emptying wheel rich with facts,

figures, this hungry mirror of *you you you*

moving you across this asphalt park
like a handicapped dancer, pressing his song

like heavy time right through the floor.

Author Profile:

Denis Stokes was born in Toronto and grew up in Scarborough. He was educated at St. Mike's, U. of T., F.E.U.T. and Vermont College (MFA).

He is the author of the chapbooks *Scarborough Poems* (Wordwrights Canada), *Dublin in the Sunlight*; *With Adam, Gathering*; *What the Street Knows* and *Peace Comes Dropping Slow* (all with Albernum Press), plus the books *Tunnel Jumping* (Scarlet Leaf Press), The Blackstock Children(Scarlet Leaf).

His work has appeared in such journals as Descant, Queen's Quarterly, Quarry, CVII, Arc and various anthologies in Canada, the U.S. and Ireland. He was the winner of the Northern Ontario Writers Award in Poetry (1995, Nipissing University). His work has been nominated for a Pushcart Prize and a National Magazine Award.

Denis has lived and taught in the GTA, northern B.C., northern Q.C. and northern Ontario, often involving students from First Nations. He has been teaching Fac. Ed. courses and Writing courses at Nipissing University. His interests include fastball and other sports (ardent fan for teams in T.O.), canoeing and hiking, the theatre and activist concerns. He organizes and hosts the Conspiracy of 3 Reading Series in North Bay, ON, one of the longest running series in Ontario.

A dual citizen of Canada and Ireland, he is married to a very patient woman, Mary, who has blessed him with four wonderfully grown-up kids.

www.ingramcontent.com/pod-product-compliance
Lightning Source LLC
Chambersburg PA
CBHW052150070526
44585CB00017B/2056